The Ambulatorium

Zak Mucha

The Ambulatorium

Published by Pay What It Costs Publishing, LLC
2023 1st Printing
ISBN: 978-0-99-685545-7
Cover art: Bridgette Bramlage

Acknowledgements:

Several of these pieces have been previously published in *Anti-Heroin Chic*; *Boredom, Horror Glory*; *Creativity and Madness, Vol. 3*; *Local Honey*; *The Harbourmaster's Loug*; *Room: A Sketchbook for Analytic Action*; *Spolia Magazine*; *Mad in America*; and *Tuck Magazine*.

For Andrew Vachss (1942-2021)

This adoption teaches the morality of
some crime and the pride in specific unemployments,

the difference between inmates and convicts,
self-affirmation in the latter's refusal

to acquiesce. In the dark, I drive back to my room
with a bag of shoes and a pocketful of cake

like a loved homeless man, bonds past blood filling
my chest and closing my throat so I cannot speak.

Table of Contents

1.

"The child's favorite and most intense occupation is play. We may perhaps say that every child at play behaves like a writer, by creating a world of his own or, to put it more correctly, by imposing a new and more pleasing order on the things that make up his world. It would therefore be wrong to think that he did not take this world of his seriously; indeed, he takes his play very seriously and expends a great deal of emotion on it. The opposite of play is not seriousness – it is reality."

--Sigmund Freud

"The trick is not minding that it hurts…"

--Peter O'Toole in *Lawrence of Arabia*

"I think the quick turn ruins us/ I used to love Big Bird/ then
I saw his n-word supercut"

--Open Mike Eagle

Front Room

A black tarp rolls down all four sides of the concrete
slab ranch, blocking out the night sky and the neighbors.

A stage set, one spotlight over the dining room
table between the crib and buffet as the

parents whisper over pencil scratch on graph paper.
Ghosts hang onto the tall grass beneath the power

lines out back and roam the front room where credit cards
are snipped in half and the good furniture kept clean.\

In daylight, the smell of fresh-cut grass signals
other lawns, each blade contributing a tiny hum

to the collective warning shared kin to kin,
acknowledging the ultimate concern.

The Leopard-Spotted Bear

During the nights across a childhood something
happens, turning each and all into strangers.

In the mornings they always looked the same except
a tiny, altered piece -- an eyelid crease, a tic –

signified a break in continuity since
sundown. Once, in the middle of the night, I saw

a leopard-spotted bear lumbering through the house,
his dark underside disappearing him as he

rose to scratch his back against the door jamb by the
kitchen phone. Sometimes months passed between the switches

but these incremental disconnections warned me
to the somnambulant lookalikes of daylight.

*

Lights would flash and roll outside my bedroom window
in the gangway between houses on the switch nights.

New family members kept replacing those from
the day before, each a bit more foreign than

the last. Over time, I learned others came before me.
I had an older brother I never met and

my little brother got switched forty-seven times
before starting high school. By then, we were drinking

dad's Old Style with our cereal before class, our
conversation nothing more than an intricate

series of grunts and shrugs. The neighbors watched us wait
for the bus like each morning was coincidence.

*

Traces of shared memory splintered with every
switch, each replacement knew less than the one before.

Divergence in linking metastasized. No one's
hair looked right. Holidays, anniversaries, and

birthdays were guided by sets of abandoned scripts
that would never haunt the next household set.

The school lunch lady let me into the older
kids' library for books of the 19th century

demons and 1970's poltergeists. There were no
revenants and no one came back. The neighbors'

dogs howled and jumped their fences to attack when
the later versions of my dad mowed the lawn.

A Pink Safeway Sky

The fried chicken counter holds shovels and salt for
quarantine winter. At the gas station bar stool

a triple-book long haul trucker plays video
poker under a yellowed note: “Entertainment

purposes only” -- payouts are for regulars,
like liquid benzo derivatives on Reddit

sold and labeled: “For research purposes only --
not for human consumption.” Past the pumps the pink

night sky looks inside-out and the streets are empty
like the rapture came just as John of Patmos said

it did and we missed it, busy keeping three books --
one for the boss, one for the cops, one for real time.

The Crime of the Century
(via Maurice Sendak)

The children were always falling out the window or
between the cars or off the front page headlines.

All life hung from a structuring absence, even
the dog left a goodbye note: "I won't be coming back."

Grandmother dressed him all in white and stood him
on the porch to ward off God's envy as death had

to be tricked over and over again. These curses
carried in whispers which survived American

pogroms and Ellis Island holding cells could be
undone by the ungrateful child. In adulthood,

a boy's wordless signifiers waited for the
pages to be drawn, stolen children in every book.

*

No one believed he saw the child's shadowed body
among the gray leaves when he himself was a boy.

No one believed he saw the blonde hair black in the
afternoon edition newsstand rack, that baby

found at the edge of the Hopewell property even after
the postcards arrived assuring his life.

With newsreel transatlantic solo flights and health
tips from Jafsie an entire country sought to

ward off the evil eye, each contributing to
the whole of a culture protecting itself with

white people voodoo and awaiting news of the
cemetery meeting with some dark foreigner.

*

The last watercolors of his brother floating
away in footsie pajamas, mourned not stolen.

Every other image a doppelganger
of those who weighted him with a survivor's guilt

as he worked over a lightboard with one eye
covered and accommodating a shaky hand,

validating a child's dread of the adults'
complicity and the love of a brother with

branches for arms to wrap him in the forest and
sleep together buried in blossoms, both knowing

there are no wet nurses keeping a baby safe
at sea and ladders can be cut from any old wood.

The Center of the World
(thanks to City Cave Zen sangha)

In the bruised sky of an Arizona monsoon
a hand, white-gloved like Mickey Mouse, points down

at one house among the pebbled yards squared by walks
and driveways where a girl runs loops from eaves to curb

in a stinging rain that by its absence defines
the arroyos, buzzing like the plume of cicadas

that came before. The other white-gloved hand points
to a mechanic in Chicago looking at

a marriage proposal writ in graffiti script
across a green dumpster in the alley. Between

the hands, a paleteria man pushing his cart
can see gold teeth chewing at the edge of the clouds.

*

That marriage proposal written on the dumpster:
"I love you, bitch. Will you marry me? – Onions"

with full punctuation and placed strategically
along the route between her mom's and the Chinese

place that's not as good as Wing Ho used to be,
filled with cops clanking around for carry-out at

the register. Our own selfishness dismisses
the eternal beauty of all dead religions

and demands immortality so as to not
end like the Manicheans who ate only melons,

were slaughtered by the Romans, and whose last scrap of
dogma has long turned black against the light of day.

Jokes and Their Relation to the Unconscious

The host of a 1965 Friday night
horror show sits silent at a poker table

of sidekicks broadcasting live between movie clips
and car lot commercials. He orders, "Let me think..."

and they all hold stone still, a circle of goons
imitating Rodan's *Thinker* for a full

sixty seconds, an oil painting on TV
during the *Attack of the 50-Foot Woman*.

The sacred is defined simply as that which is
not profane. And F. Scott Fitzgerald suggested

writers should never use exclamation points
because it's like laughing at your own jokes.

The Ambulatorium

Dark as Esau, the rough god wakes up to throw
another empty head into the lake. The village

is asleep, a few fishermen see ripples reach
their lines. Skulls found after the thaw go unmentioned

but the increased workload earns complaints. Wilhelm Reich
teaches farm girls at the clinic it's all normal,

his magic blankets and boxes almost ready.
When the carnival comes through town, the sheriff

confiscates trailer hitches. If you all want to
leave, you have to make your nut.

An empty cage is a waste of resources and
we pride ourselves on fiscal responsibility.

A Bear Cub Stares at the American Caste System

Dad takes the boy to the edge of the village
where the bear cub is chained to a tree. Uncle has

the camcorder and men from the truck yard follow
with flasks and bottles. The boy in his best white

track suit leads the flannelled and windburned animals,
their bellies hard and thickened against the weather.

A Saturday morning where something is to be
left in the woods, something new brought home.

Prayers to Allah and a will produced by
paternal devotion assures the boy will always

be protected along the path to pay-per-view
in the U.S., with the cub as proud as the men.

*

Twenty years later, a perfect record with no
endorsement deals or color commentary jobs

because he has the wrong god – the plane-crashing,
marathon-bombing, explosive-vest-wearing,

cave-living, savage god that sits on a dirt floor
and eats with his hands. Retiring from the cage

he keeps his promise to his mother as they have
rich men at home who know the blond American

god will never see them as white. Everyone will
be ranked according to their deeds. God will repay

them in full for what they have done and his boy will
not be disqualified by the curl of his tongue.

**There Used to be Communism,
But Now There's Just God.**

A mourning son in the Ukraine forest strapped
the kitchen door to his back despite the soldiers'

orders to evacuate without any
potentially irradiated personal property or soil.

Officials denied any accident and deemed
protective gear unmasculine. Drunk soldiers

clearing villages were fed a roasted house pet
in one dovetailed act of subversion and grieving.

The son heard the old man's ghost whispering praise from
the dying grasses as he ran from the warning shots,

the cooling board that carried his father from the
deathbed to the grave, a cloak across his shoulders.

The Meat Empire

The sausage king of Moscow was found zip-tied and
run through with bolts like St. Sebastian in bed.

Impatient extortionists let his girlfriend slip
away to collect her cut after they ditch the

car and crossbow and do something with the other
guy they left drugged and cuffed to the bed in their flat.

We search for signs of forward movement something to
anticipate the time and portions doled out.

One last job, just like they say in the movies,
to reach the land of Crown Royal bikini tops

shopping mall lots filled with camouflaged Hum-vees,
and Jason Statham movies that have a sense of humor.

Ghazals for Cook County Jail

The Tennessean with chains tattooed around each wrist,
bicep inked with the limestone brick of Joliet

where bats halo the tower, reads James Patterson
with *A Million Little Pieces* waiting between

his commissary flip flops. When told the trauma
memoir was fiction, the author busted in Oprah's

pastel courtroom, he said, "Good for him. Hope he
made some money off it. Shit's all the same, anyway."

Both writers marketed themselves well enough to
make TV and the Cook County Jail book cart

simultaneously where the ink of
paperbacks and tattoos mark time.

*

That was the year of 11,000 inmates and
five escape attempts, one made as a guard claimed

soapy water was thrown in his face, rendering him
helpless as a five-year old in the bath.

The Tennessean's case waited patiently,
the liquid cough in his chest minding time.

"Fucking Oprah." Four syllables said with the
belligerence of a defaulted hometown

that lies about its work history, bragging of
men's jobs that don't exist. Two words said with the scorn

of the last first-shift taverns -- a sneer that paints a
lawn jockey in blackface to challenge the neighbors.

*

That house sank like a barge, those man-and-wife
months a dream interrupting a line of shared bunks,

barracks, and flophouse rooms. Lock-ups and landlords.
Power respects nothing but its own ideal self.

At the Starr Hotel, Tennessee woke for a shape up
and just missed Speck getting caught for those nurses,

then met again in Statesville where Speck enjoyed his
celebrity, transitioning topless with breasts

and a blonde bowl cut, camcorders, coke, and black boys
everywhere. "It's all show business," -- that's what the

Marine Corps MP said about Vietnam when
he hauled Tennessee stateside in well-oiled cuffs.

The Child Watching TV, 1977

Remember that one Three Stooges where Larry was
trying to figure out whether man was good with

evil tendencies or the other way around
while stuffing a turkey for the rich folks' party.

It was the only episode with a voice-over --
a low growl buried in the UHF hiss,

describing the 80,000 shadows left on
the walls and men with ghost sleeves walking into

the sea after Nagasaki. He could have been
a Zen priest like Buster Keaton trained not to laugh

if it weren't for the other two pounding
each other's skulls with hammers night and day.

*

Awaiting the swat of the big rubber fish that
would send him and his little hat end over end,

the child billed as "The Little Boy Who Can't Be
Damaged" felt the whispered threat like an arm-grab --

the crowds laughed when he didn't. As an adult he
held his composure as houses fell around him,

a resigned stillness perched on the piston of
a locomotive heading west an inch above

the horizon, wondering if loyalty was
locked until death or to be renewed with each turn.

This hard work of showing nothing while seeking the
perfection nestled in the language of adults.

*

A found book of slate prayers – Sonny Liston and
Spahn Ranch and Dick Hickock – whispered the country's sad

history, offering a route from a house of
ghosts and genogram myths luminescing under

the blue light of the TV. A finger pointing
to the same moon that watched Dock Ellis throwing

a no-hitter for the Pirates with a head full
of LSD. A game played before the child's birth,

made real as a dream space by his desire
to embrace that terrified joy of the unknown,

to say: "Let's see how this goes," laughing, as the infield
rolls like an immense turfed ocean beneath his feet.

The Red Line Home

Cheese puff orange fingertips and grape pop. White Owl blunts,
soft-pack Newports, and keychain mace for the walk home.

Her boyfriend the bouncer gave her a boxcutter
and zip ties just in case. The el car passes where

Maryville juvie shelter used to be and she
knows the lake stays on your left when you elope south.

A residential program tattoo freehanded
between her shoulder blades says LOVE LIFE above a

compass rose with east and west transposed. Social
workers took them both when brother burned down the house

with a propane torch on a Sunday night and she
saw a newly christened ship set out to sea.

On Smoking

Unwrap a talisman to ward off the unknown
a ceremony to deny the need for prayers,

a refusal of the gravitational pull
toward the most democratic aspect of life.

The exhale a veil between myself and the world,
a symptom that keeps and curses the same promise.

A little red box, tin-edged and glass-fronted
cellophane wrapped with a tiny axe inside --

in case of emergency, break glass. Even our ghost
smoked Lucky Strikes in the basement trying to find

a way back into the group and we are all
amateur firefighters standing in the alley.

*

As the kid, they told me soft-pack menthols were for
black guys or cons but I stole my first ones from an

uncle who smoked while jogging. Now my corner store
offers fewer tax stamps per pack as they unload

cartons curbside between the fares. The clerks rotate
as they become Americans guarding against

shoplifters with chore boy scouring pads kept up high
and a can of loosies beneath the counter for

trusted regulars who float between transient
spaces, knowing employers and landlords are

the natural enemies of man and keep their
pockets filled since they don't know when they'll be home.

*

Refusing to accept the world as it is
I want to memorialize my own guilt and

those whom I can live without. Being driven by but
not driving a child's effort to be

accepted in quiet ways that sink deep into
the bone, patching over a suspected empty

spot, a cartoon black hole, flimsy and bottomless,
which no praise can fill. There's a vibrating urge

for motion, a frantic energy that swirls out
into nothing, seeking a guarantee against

the world and against the pull into an open space
where no ground is expected for half a second.

*

There's no boss standing over me, but Gillian
Welch echoes: "Never minded working hard,

just who I'm working for." That speaking 'I'
is never being spoken of, especially

when I say I am looking for a prayer that
would change me without such a fight. Against the

charts of money and time, logic never stands,
covered over by the geometry of

uncanny parallels and the temptation to
conclude the serenity prayer with an amen

of "fuck that." And now when I feel that pull, I try to
convince myself it's not my problem.

The Perfect Plan Finds its Own Way

Doc Pomus plows his wheelchair through the bootleggers'
sidewalk stacks of dubbed cassettes, analogue cheats

of Little Richard gospel and Magic Sam's howl. Doc,
with two shoulder holsters under his jacket because

reloading takes time, curses the thieves stealing from
the dead, curses the cheat of time's function and factor.

On his way to meet Simone Weil, healthy and full
now, a streak of gray curling at her temple to

show she has been in the world for a while. Forty
years of marriage, their hands still play as they laugh

at the thought of a bullet ricocheting for
twenty years in a breezeblock stairwell in Queens.

*

An eight hour conversation spiraling through
the deep twist of Bee-Line paperbacks and the

prison system's refusal of the Church of
the New Savior's t-bone and brandy sacrament.

This adoption teaches the morality of
some crime and the pride in specific unemployments,

the difference between inmates and convicts,
self-affirmation in the latter's refusal

to acquiesce. In the dark, I drive back to my room
with a bag of shoes and a pocketful of cake

like a loved homeless man, bonds past blood filling
my chest and closing my throat so I cannot speak.

2.

"Like movement, one has to keep going. Sin is atoned when the sinner becomes sinless not through the cessation or avoidance of sin, but by owning up to what one has done and living out its consequences. It is, as it were, actively living one's end."

--Jamieson Webster

"Yet what the memory repudiates controls the human being. What one does not remember dictates who one loves or fails to love."

--James Baldwin

"I know a man who once stole a ferris wheel."

--Dashiell Hammett

"This is America, Dog."

The freedom to justify a perspective
via the transductive logic of a child
linking status, situation, and desire
lacks the blunt compassion Marlo Stanfield
offered the security guard at the Saveland
Food Mart all hurt about those two lollypops
pocketed in the fourth season of The Wire:
"You want it to be one way
but it's the other way."

King Tubby Praxis

The intuitive fumbling for
the formula hidden in the
divine mathematics of 70s dub
where all but the bass line
drops at just the right spot is
like the barometric change of a
theater audience gasp which cannot
be forced by guilt or the cultural
capital which induces every
standing ovation.

The universe's geometry leaves some bills
unpaid and some benzo prescriptions
refilled to the last as garbage bags of
clothes pile up on the sidewalk outside the
storage lockers between the dollar store
and the planned parenthood satellite office
that's always got a broken window.

Me and my pal in Oakland want to fly
to Ireland for the astronomical odds of
a prop bet we'd place as to whether
one specific film director will get arrested
within a certain timeframe for
a specific crime because we suspect
the consistent symmetry of his shot
compositions might signify
certain felonies.

Ever Since I Was a Kid I Heard

My name said inside my ear
as a whisper or less than that.
A filament's gasp. Like it might
not have been said at all.
And deep within that quiet
is the derailing of a train,
a chorus of every deep siren
bellowing along the shore,
every piece of glass in town shattering,
a land mass tearing itself from the sea,
redrawing the history of every map
charted. A memory that can only
trace a slip, a distant edge of the event,
for all we see is nothing but
the frayed end tips of a beard and gown
and I only hear the ghost
of a neutrino whispering to me.

Copula

I remember some kid on the playground
told me human blood is not actually red.
It changes color when exposed to oxygen.
So we can never see the real color of blood.
Being smart standing in the gravel.
Watching the lunch lady in her yellow
safety vest smoking through recess.
Once we really see something,
we have changed it for good.

A copula links nouns to define
a form of being. The absence of
a thing becomes our first knowledge
of the possibilities of a self repeatedly
defined by loss and want.

To be aware of the sea by a gentle push
toward the water or by the suffocating lack
of being yanked into the sunlight
by jawbone and flesh.

On the Thorndale platform hands full
with a donut and coffee, paper and cup
trademarked pink and orange,
each wrist ringed with bandages
since dirtied by days at home with
the left still cuffed in white laminate
with dot-matrix printed names,
last and first
and date-of-birth.

Almost Ordinary Time

Heading west out of Lansing
early with the rental shadow
cutting a slit in the sunlit pavement
a compass pointing home
with a car half empty
on December 26th

Motina

A ghost moves through the flickering contrast
of security camera footage which the third shift
never monitors. She carries the subtracted weight
of a hardbound notebook, the soft pages torn
from their stitches and discarded so sky can
be painted on the heavy stock binding, wet blue
dabbed away with napkin or sleeve
to make a cloud.

She sneaks dollar store desserts from her daughter
into the staff lounge at 3 AM. Supplementing cold
coffee with the cracked stale circus peanuts and
cut ropes of soft black licorice arranged in opposing
troop formations on the borderless formica landscape
protecting towns of sugar packets and creamer cups
from a feigned confusion of tongues.

On her side all the pit bulls in their coats and
booties wait down in the subway until the bombing
stops and one of their people returns from telling
an occupying soldier to fill his pockets with sunflower
seeds so he can fertilize the town square
and his bones will see the sky.

The Workshop

On a low shelf rests a menagerie of glass
hammers trapping translucent pink skies
and clouds of aquarium green each one
perfectly balanced an inch and a half
from the head, each one promising two
strikes to sink any nail, each one
demanding respect from a world
that will continue without them.

The Other Weird Birds of Rome

Sliding black fingerprints across the glass
above the city before coming home
from a day in the olive groves they slide
down with sleeper cell orchestration
filling trees, closing streets, and burying
cars in an oil-slick pulp of tiny Rorschach
tests, a murmuration footprint
for cobblestone and travertine.

From a Hotel Lobby Picture Book

The walled city of Kowloon
seen from the sky as
a tumor of concrete and rebar
corrugated tin and laundry lines
facing the sea with its spine
to the mountains balanced between
colonized land and criminalized lives.

Six PM, Via Salaria

A whippet mounts his vespa
at the curb, fits his helmet,
clicks his chin, lights a smoke,
and makes the sign of the cross
before diving into the imagined
space between moving cars.

Lacan

Chomsky said the man was a charlatan
just fucking with the crowd, but spot on
saying the turbine both is and is
not powered by the holy spirit.

He liked to scream this while running
between the cars when traffic was heavy and slow.
He knew he'd have to wait on some corner
for his ride to catch up eventually

and hear the whisper of some absent tongue,
despite the failure of language that can't
be nailed down like Christ, leaving us each with
an empty spot as signifiers keep

sliding across objects. And him simply trying
to get laid with that yellow turtleneck.

Metonymy

The unsupervised toddler
with her mouth full of
grandma's costume jewelry
kept safe in a box blooming with
ladybugs, bumblebees, and pairs
of deep black plums tangled in gold
strands and flash-frozen constellations:
One marker of the family covenant
where, for three generations,
to speak of need is crazy
and the crazy are ignored
and those ignored
are left to chance
staggering on new muscles
toward the stairs.

The Wolf-Man's Hand

With the first dark blushes of transformation
the wolf-man's hand places a silent
and detachable cherry light, a flashing
red swivel like in the old cop shows,
right on the front windowsill.

In broad daylight the doorbell camera
records the driver documenting his drop-off --
a preventive strike against customer complaints
when a signature is required -- since
every docked minute is another
spec of fuel for a trip to the moon.

When night clouds close the sky again
and all the neighbors' packages are inside,
the sirens screwed into his eaves wait
to alert the whole block
as to who else feels that pull.

A good neighbor knows the irrecusable
responsibility to the other, a perpetual
conversation of undiscovered process
and impossible debt.

Slipping Away from Zazen

I was working a garage sale
in black and white, trying to teach
two young men how to negotiate
with a customer who was clearly
an elderly Harpo Marx, long retired
without his costume or his brothers.
He was making a wordless, lonely, fuss
over the masking-taped prices
which were, clearly, non-negotiable.

The Dead Sea Figures

After the agricultural revolution
perfect math told us we could get ten rabbits from
just two every four months. On the spiral of
sacred geometry every point is a

constellation strung with its own interior
blossoms of Fibonacci coordinates each
gently holding the Koan: "There is nothing
I dislike." The Dead Sea retreats four feet

every year, drawing down to the statues of
Hildegard de Bingen and Charles Mingus
standing in the center mud, their crowns far from
the waterline. A psychoanalyst in Tehran

recently said something wonderful must have
happened to Duke Ellington when he came through
Isfahan because he changed the name of that song.
And she said American blues always holds

the potential of falling from melancholy
into mourning with the turn of the next line.

Milk Teeth

The baby teeth of John the Baptist
saved in a little clay pot for they knew
he would take to the woods and find
a new father to walk him
the rest of the way.

With duties beyond his own breath
he offered his neck to the soldiers
so his kid could keep his own
for a little while longer.

What remains is one adult molar
levitating in a tiny space housed
in gold-framed crystal coveted by
a neurosurgeon in Thibodeaux
who also owns a shotgun-shell
pistol and a sliver of saintly wrist bone.

On Not Being Able to Paint

The winged ox of St. Luke was buried
with liturgical combs and whale bones
in the same years they painted Mary
holding a middle-aged baby
with the face of a cable news
economist who looked like a
nightmare-exhausted nine-year-old
who kept everything to himself.
By the time the ox was exhumed
the middle-aged baby was replaced by
the erotic load of dead Jesus with
his ribs open across Mary's lap
and the producers kept the old
economist on file as he never
refused a prime TV segment.

King Herod Bail Bonds

The imagined Yeshua who somehow
has plans for an America not yet
existing on any symbolic or
imaginary register would be
the same type to have his boys take out the
zealot who baptized him, leaving John face
down in a grove instead of scratching days
on the wall before leaving his flock of
mud-caked whirling dervishes waiting
with an open call for a new prophet.
No one's niece dances well enough to fill
that plate, not even in a New York City
where Lazarus returned somewhere in
nineteen hundred and seventy-five
like the song says.

Yeshua in Tyler, Texas – Spring 2022

Flattened by camera crew lights against a night sky
the house painter answers questions between bites of
ice cream, his flip tooth safe in his front pocket
so as to not swallow it again. His van idling
against the six-lane suburban sprawl
of Texas, the cop wanted to know
where they all were going. The house painter
said the strip club didn't serve food
like some others do and one of the guys
in back is too young and they're all
excited to be in the city, but a pick-up crew,
one's from Arkansas, another a carpenter
from somewhere else but he can probably paint.

Hiding in the back of an unfinished work van
in Tyler, Texas which is all nursing homes and
chain restaurants and tire shops, He risked
still being taken for John's reincarnation
like a copycat serial killer who, instead of
making his own name, inadvertently extends
the legend of the original, foreclosing on his own
name. And the goof with the ice cream talking to
the cops and TV crew helping Him to figure this
all out. Black and brown girls disappear by the
dozens in silence and white girls who go gone
get their own podcasts. And in Tyler they close
the to-go margaritas with zip-ties but
in Louisiana they leave the paper end
on the straw and trust you to be responsible.

The guys stayed huddled back in the van disappointed
one was too young for the club, another wanting a meal
with his stripper, the others too drunk to enjoy or care
while the driver happy to be innocent of any concerns
with his ice dream, chatting with a cop right on the
yellow line catching the lights of the strip malls chain
restaurants and box stores taking everyone's money
like the girls in the clubs promising nothing.

The Magic Trick

You pull away the bark of a tree branch for the sheet music
below and the find the history of a city in matchbook covers
and flat faces of comic strip characters. All for a crowd
chanting to become impossible ahistorical subjects unable
to place themselves as landmarks become homogeneous
and we search the internet to see what building once were
on that corner where the mattress store used to be.
Stories that could be shared were meant to keep us safe.
There was once a Jesus dog on butcher paper c-list celebs
kept buying and sending back because it was too much to have
in their homes as it also erased linear time and narrative.
Think about it -- a Doberman being born with those tattoos.

3.

"But the only place I can live is always the present; there is, therefore, no value in what I can remember about my past except that I cannot forget what I cannot remember. Consequently, unless I know what the past is that fills my mind, I cannot forget it; and I am not paying attention to the present if I am obsessed with the future which I know nothing about because it has not yet happened."

--Wilfred R. Bion

"Our clocks, silverware, crystal vases, and fancy china were exchanged for bacon, lard, sausages, and such things. Once an old gypsy man wanted my father's top hat. It didn't even fit him. With that hat down over his eyes, he handed over a live duck."

--Charles Simic

Pick Poor Robin Clean

Geeshie Wiley slit her second husband's throat
in Houston one year after she recorded

"Last Kind Word Blues" up in Wisconsin and posed
for her partner, L.V., one foot on the running

board like Bonnie Parker, legs open defiant
between a hem and high boots before she slipped off

like a ghost in the seams, undocumented but
for six songs buried in a static of misheard

lines of gnostic praise -- either "my babe" or "my face"
for what she can see across the wide river

and her father's last words blurred just where to send
his body if the Germans killed him in the war.

*

Born twenty-fourth of twenty-five children
without the day marked by law, Sonny Liston heard

Geeshie chanting beneath the dirt, when he was
in the fields. Hornets drowned out the chant in the ring.

Patterson couldn't look him in the eye and
fell, accepting the punches that could cause cancer.

He came up relieved, the pressure gone, snuck out of
Comiskey in a fake beard and Liston went home

to an empty airport terminal as the new champ,
knowing JFK would set the dogs out on him

rather than shake his hand. He would always be
the stick-up man wearing yellow plaid and no mask,

with swollen hands of leathered cement and wrists thick
with blood as he skips rope to "Night Train" on repeat.

*

Born dead Sonny wanted them to know how he felt,
but even when he won, they got to return to life.

In Las Vegas the chanting was replaced by
the sound of one freight train clicking heavy and slow.

The last Pullman porters heard the lines sung between
the cars, coming up from the tracks those last kind words

a debt and legacy that cannot be paid off
or accepted cleanly by parent or child.

Called from Saturn to be reborn Sun-Ra returned
with a cosmology to be mimeographed

and distributed between sets, instructions for
a better planet and a gospel for poor Charles.

Ghazals for Fat Possum Records

They ran out of North Mississippi bluesmen grown
old with swollen ankles, bad hearts, and diabetes,

shirtless in their front yards, cigarettes dangling,
posing as if they didn't give a damn or as

if they didn't know any eyes were on them. Or
as if they had no say or as if maybe they

were in on the white boys' opportunism long
after the first waves of dry recitations.

R.L. slipped from the hospital like Lazarus
calling for a wire transfer to the casino.

More white boys who couldn't sit behind the beat
brought the first Theremin to Oxford screaming drunk.

*

One Rockerfeller cannot feed a whole tribe.
R.L. reimagined trickster tales of late-night,

pajama-clad, panic attacks shared by Hitler
and Tojo hiding with their heads in paper sacks.

And a little monkey, who was actually
the probation officer, forcing his way into

the bigger animals' party, badge hidden, with
a front pocket of whiskey and a ass pocket of gin.

The student's watch and glasses were left behind on
an old canoe, his dissertation in his dorm room,

a signal to Mom buried in the scratches of
open note hillbilly music before the war.

*

She responded with a quarter-million dollar
reward for information on her boy. Fortune

hunters and documentarians paralleled
the shore as arrows plinked the water. Customer

survey cards would fall from Fat Possum packaging,
questions mocking embedded race and class issues:

"Where at you get this?" "Where you stay?" "How much money
you make?" And above an empty rectangle, the

instruction: "Trace your house key in this box." The joke
died with R.L., leaving British aristocrats

to simulate music of the antebellum
south on Jumbotron screens in exchange for your rent.

Sigmund Freud Classic Comics "What If" Issue

When he was just a boy, the Wolfman asked
his nurse whether Jesus had a bottom like him.

Not this one shining bright without a spot of dirt
or a drop of blood on Him, who would end up

a short hundred years later, doing two shows
daily in the room off of the cruise ship buffet,

singing "Frankie and Albert" before caught aware
of himself, silent for an hour between songs

like William Burroughs as a special guest calling
bingo in a nursing home, his pistol in his lap,

or Alastair Crowley at a short yellow light in his triangle
hat and his fists in his eyes.

The Stowaway

A total pro, she denied everything and stuck
to her story: She didn't want to see places and

had no need to go anywhere. Nurses peeked
under her tongue twice a day and she got to keep

the paper cups to build a radio tower
for her nightstand. Case managers called out games of

courtroom bingo to prepare them all for trial –
the bailiff is C4, the judge is always D5.

You give enough right answers, you get to go home.
The TV stays off until Feelings Worksheets are done.

Mandatory compliance always crumbles when
the threat of pleasure or punishment is withdrawn.

*

Shipped back to Cook County with the lines memorized
and the promise of Remorse, Repent, and Release

between her teeth: I'm Sorry and I Won't Do It
Again. Can I Go Now? The destinations are

random and the desire to be elsewhere is not
hers, not like those measuring themselves against what

they can buy and eat between the gates, flying
because they have somewhere else to be. She becomes

everywhere in that stomach drop when gravity
pulls heavy against her body in the lift and tilt.

The components of her only self dissolve like
smoke, a silent moment she is absent and whole.

*

She sees the car lots and forest preserves hiding
the giant gears buried deep in the earth, she sees

the wing tracing a line laid before anyone
was here. Like she knew the static and last blip of

the cathode tube TV clicking off was God saying
Hello, to reach that she had to perform unseen,

as security cameras found, delicate
pirouettes past cops with their Starbucks cups and

through TSA agents dreaming of their own guns.
She thinks of the poor stewardess in the poem,

sucked out the door mid-flight, and how there's no
right answers, just some lucky moments of floating.

Night Studio
(for Philip Guston)

I am certain he dreamt of car crashes. Painting
chain-smoking Klansmen in cartoon convertibles

he brought himself into the world. A dark line to
pull the horizon to the corners of the room

for the signifiers of cigarette, lightbulb,
canvas, clock, and worker's shoe. The Roman hands and

feet of giants made flesh again. One heavy eye
looks for itself in the hardbound books cut open

like slabs of meat. Fractured self-portraits painted by
the fist of brushes sleeping next to him with the

bed sheets pulled up and window shades pulled down. One old
friend saw the new work and never spoke to him again.

*

I am certain he dreamt the still-life of nighttime
crashes, ambulance strobes lighting the puddles of

rain and glass and the wrinkles of metal across
double yellow dashes leading upstate. Back then

no fiberglass or airbags and each hospital
bed had an ashtray. In the morning he painted

the room pink, then black, and pink again,
replacing clouds with cave paintings, mythology, and dirty

jokes. A wrist descending from an impure sky
is the hand of god striking a match on dry earth.

I am certain Picasso never smart-mouthed the
soldiers over Guernica like they say he did.

Slow Train Coming

The PBS news broadcaster after forty-some
years in the business pulls off her rubber face,

skull and wig, exposing a tiny lizard head
peeking out from her modestly collared blouse

and says in a deep baritone, “Well, I just thought
you all should know,” before the market report

updates segue into the arts and culture segment.
Though not ideal, this might be manageable.

Balance is not necessarily a good thing,
all those stumbling eruptions none can see

tell us the importance of the relationships
wherein we lose our equilibrium.

Composite Sketch with Multiple Witnesses

The tribal descendants of Charles Lindberg and
William Pierce sunk their fiber optic lines down to

the empty throne at the bottom of the ocean,
the vacant seat gathering coral ever since

John of Patmos got locked up. Men waiting for those
burnished bronze feet to break the shore like cargo ships

where wind will bend and strip the trees bare, revolving
the grays of ocean and sky for one moment

before the aluminum-sided wood-frame
houses are broken to shivers and sent drifting,

certain in their fantasy that Jesus is a
Navy Seal calling them each to watch his six.

*

The most recent shooter emptied a bank of humans,
left the money, and called the cops on himself for

the suicide standoff. Still on probation as
a prison guard trainee, his Wisconsin ID

proofs the phenotype of babyfat profile and abandoned
crew cut signifying the lack

epigenetically camouflaged, holding
a constellation of half-verbalized grudges

snarled in knots behind his eyes. The anxiety hum of
those fragmented narratives leave him

walking a loop like a sick dog trotting himself
to bone, repetition buried deep past wishes.

*

Been here since forever: the kid in the basement,
the long-distance hauler with three sets of mileage

logs –discretionary measures of time and distance--
and the Coast Guard clerk who never clears his browser.

Creeping the periphery, the isolato
who lives a simulation until the last day:

Shooting up a yoga studio in a mall
or following his ex to the office again,

each simultaneously victim and victor,
perpetually happening and never existing,

justified by his silence which protects him from
shame while waiting for an echo and a mirror.

*

The Smartest Kid on Earth, sits with his cereal
as the auto-show Superman tip-toes plain clothes

from Mom's room, leaving the boy with a message and
a gift. Jimmy, wearing his hero's mask when she

wakes and happily missing the Oedipal joke, goes:
"Mom! He said to tell you he had a real good time!"

A boy could learn to kill from the back page ads where
Count Dante's two-finger technique – Dim Mak,

the death touch – was offered next to x-ray glasses
revealing bones and underwear, minotaur seed

packets, a dollar for a bowl of sea monkeys who
who promised to come to life in the comic books.

*

The grocery store cashier with her ashtray and
Tab sits behind the cage, cashing checks from memory

and keeping cartons of Mom's ultra-slims locked up
with the liquor, arguing with Dad every time.

The spinning wire rack flashes a dollar double-issue:
Superman in the ring with Muhammad Ali

and dumbbell Batman sitting in the audience
for a lame story where these is no chance of death.

Count Dante, a south side Chicago Irishman
was a part-time hairdresser with vague mob ties.

He also, allegedly, hid in the toilet
during the 1970 dojo wars.

*

Charles Whitman climbed the tower with a shelled
half-pecan of a tumor nestled behind his eyes,

setting the precedent of killing the women
at home before heading to campus. Presented

as the anomaly, his organicity
protected the other end of the spectrum where

selling rifles for cash out of a car trunk at
a gun show or from a box store parking lot is

one's God-given right to make a little extra
and not screw up one's disability payments

or set off court monitors about income for
child support because she'd just waste on herself.

*

Analog entertainment, Bee-line paperbacks,
and clip-job true crime pulps birthed serial killer

celebrity. Focus on the Family sold
VHS tapes of Bundy's last interview and

offered legal assistance since he found Christ
and blamed pornography on his way out the door.

Suburban California sex magick fired the
first NASA rockets into the empty desert,

setting up the question whether we wanted
to be part of the crime or part of the punishment,

imagining free will a grand separation
from all, not the duty of one miniscule speck.

*

Roof and Rodger left manifestos for their
imagined audiences, stepping from a crowd

half federal informants, half true believers
who never paid their monthly dues. They said because

maybe a girl left them, or Mom's black boyfriend,
or because the absent father who didn't bother.

They claimed a foregone birthright to power unearned,
their missives the evidence of an infant's needs.

Mark David Chapman consoled himself so fiercely
his crib crossed the room inch by inch every night.

He dreamt of being a child god with villages
tucked in bedsheet landscapes, asking for his mercy.
*

We would be offered our own seats among the slurred
grumblings of how awful "they" are – in the truck yard,

the back yard, and from the other end of the bar where
the guy watches himself talking in the mirror,

giving instructions for the eggshell fragility
no keto or ju jitsu regimen could temper –

a locus of control inverted, allowing
the fantasy of vengeful martyrdom to break

the loop of a terrified child's magical
thinking. Safe in tautologies linked together

and nullifying each other to keep the kid
from that unknown space created by two people.

*

All razor-necked and side parted variations
of chinless blonde boys with bowl haircuts, cradling their

semi-autos and claiming allegiance to the
fantasy of an identity crystallized

by their last act and just as American as
the first forty-dollar bill of the Union.

On Ruination Day, the 14th of April,
the iceberg broke and the Okies fled and

the Great Emancipator took a bullet
in the back of the head. Apophenia means

each of us determines the links between events
and God moves on the water like coincidence.

*

Desperate men searching for the language to
explain how they have been cheated by the world,

a con built of unspoken ghosts and grudges
so that language itself becomes the barrier

separating each from all until history
protects the silence of men terrified to be seen.

November 23rd, the anniversary
of JFK's death, is also the birthday of

Billy the Kid -- fictions purified by violence
in that space where destruction creates a linking,

an understanding lasting a millisecond
then it's gone and sunk to the bottom of the sea.

Wilfred Bion's Big Russian Hat

My sister of celestial monochord, not
blood, told her eight-year-old girl she and I, this new

godfather, met when we were smaller than her. A
breath of silence allowed my sister to hold a

mind opening to the flickering sense of
mom as a child, an unknowing stranger with the

same hands, time existing before birth, and a convex
pool of infinite dark, dotted and swirling deep blue

opening across the ceiling to devour the house.
On returning, the girl asked, "Was he always bald?"

For a goodbye gift, she draws my wife in a princess
dress and me with dark crazy eyes.

LIVE PD

We watch through night vision cameras of dirty
green aquarium glass as cops in tactical

gear crunch toward a sleeping suburban house. In real
life, only 2% of all police calls end

in arrest. On TV, it's 95%.
Two squares of white blink awake above the mouth of

porch and eaves. One long leg and glowing white shoe reaches out,
then another, and the young man follows them,

dropping silently to the yard, bounding over
sidewalk and blacktop, barely tapping the ground,

like a young deer pulled forward by this uncanny
weight of new antler buds sprouting behind his eyes.

The Truth
(thanks to Dr. Joel Dvoskin)

A picture frame and a crucifix made from
origami Pall Mall packs reminds me of when

you could smoke in prison, sneak white bread and cheese
slices under your shirt to burn on your bunk with

the honeycomb of rolled milk cartons lit with a
contraband Bic ignored by the guards who hated

the warden so and snuck blades from the metal shop
to, each week, trim a tiny bit from the tip of

his walking cane before the man began questioning
the length of his limbs and the heel of his shoe and,

on some nights, what his mother ever intended
for him until the head shrink broke the bad news.

Joseph Campbell Bites the Brim Off His Hat

A blind man scratching the steps with his cane, a rock
in the swirl of tourists, girl guides, and Mormon scouts.

A modest cross and chalice leads them up the hill to Sacre Coeur
where vending machines offer commemorative coins --

a choice between one of three popes
like Bushman in Mold-o-Rama wax.

Downhill Americans take turns twerking
for camera phones against the bronze bust of Dalida

her breasts shined to gold by thirty years of hands
wishing themselves luck despite Edith Piaf's last words:

"Every damn thing you do in this life,
you have to pay for."

The Fly

The patron saint of second place checks his numbers on
Wednesdays and Saturdays, knowing end times come

gently with soft thuds at twilight in fields where
men jump from barn gables to meet The Man mid-air.

Just one fly was a surprise last night. That guy should
have been covered head-to-toe within the hour,

choking from bees born in his mouth like Candyman,
while a rain of black frogs dot the studio floor.

Jesus could have stepped on stage, shaking the Buddha's
other sandal from his crook like clicking batteries

into a sock, ready to sift wheat from
the tares right before the cameras cut away.

Another Mysterium Tremendum

The can marked "tea" holds salt, tea bags are in the one
for "sugar", and a third for coffee is empty.

An unseen pattern emerges and fades like a
kitchen rearranged by the Zodiac Killer,

an ontological categorization
of inanimate objects. The sacred tree of

a flyspeck village on the counter links heaven
and hell, holding a point of the numina to

shift the profane landscape. I cannot find my cup.
A ghost hides the spoons. The coffee pot weeps like

an icon, and we are grateful we cannot know
each other outside the sliver of space our thoughts share.

The Greenpoint YMCA Two Minutes Before Full Gentrification

A sleeping room with a toilet down the hall
was my sketchy compensation for illegal

construction work preparing the basements down
under the bridges for all those coming who had

better plans than me. I kept a closed loop before
your autumn visit, hanging drywall and writing

on spec with no space sanctified as my own with
three months down as all other squares were spoken for,

renamed, and promised away. You tolerated
the roll-up front window and storefront basement view.

I stuffed the walls with green bricks of rat poison
so you didn't have the same dreams as me.

*

The Italian bakery cases hinted at
a joy like a hypnogogic vision

of a city harbor filled with toy ducks, the chaos
of a celebration that flickers away into sleep.

You came along to the Odditorium of
wax figures, human heads from pathology labs,

serial killer confessions and autographs
for the interview. Joe Coleman worked a two-hair

brush, unaware the rage he sought out inch by inch
to define was, right then, learning to fly airplanes.

In a year he would be thrown into the present,
breathing glass and concrete from across the river.

*

Jehovah's Witnesses hummed beneath the streets,
popping up two by two with tracts and backpacks

like ants dressed to work family casual restaurants.
If a spade turned the concrete, there's be thousands

all impervious to the new millennium
and the dangers of compulsive record keeping

when real journalists start coming around,
following the tunnels all the way upstate.

I could get a sliver of my reflection in
an inside page byline at the bodega stand

and a coffee poured with dissociative precision
in the white and blue paper cups like on TV.

*

You went back to Chicago. I went back to work.
Three of the Bulgarians slept at the job site

where we built out allegedly soundproof music
studios, marking floors and hanging sheetrock with

all the planning and substance of a treehouse fort,
adding walls as security deposits cleared.

The Bulgarians' favorite joke: We work with
cigarette in one hand, Russians with vodka in

other hand, Polacks with cigarette in one hand and
vodka in the other -- that's how you can tell.

When the fire marshal demanded the permits
everyone climbed up and out the windows like rats.

*

I took showers at the Greenpoint YMCA
in those last few blocks patrolled by piano-legged

women waddling like pigeons in housedresses with cotton
candy hairdos under clear plastic babushkas.

A bearded Russian wearing a cigarette smoke
mustache watched me fumbling in the gym

at the leather teardrop bag, one arm a hammer
and the other a windshield wiper. No hum

in the wrists and elbows that could not find
the economy of weightless movement. Without

language he presented the geometry of
kinetics in a mirror of elbows and eyes.

*

The Russian pointed to his eyes, then mine, then to
the silver clasp of the teardrop. He tapped once,

a piston at his elbow, clean and effortless,
with his eyes shut. He counted four, moving the bag

slow for me: hit one, back two, front three, back four, and
hit on one again. Then he walked away, all done.

Before heading off to Bagdad, my friend told me
it'd be five years before the city felt like home

and I wanted the belonging she carried even
when the war started. She learned when the lights go out

in a café, you can tell who the spooks are
because they will always have flashlights ready.

*

Having learned two things, I began packing boxes
of books to ship UPS back to Chicago.

A sleeping bag on the floor and an answering
machine that left the first welcome home message from

a bluesman's wife: "Here's a story—that son of a
bitch. I took all his guns and all his guitars. Why

don't you write about that?" When the planes hit, I was in
the day room of a locked juvie facility

with one who played Russian Roulette with neighbor kids
and twins who slept in a box truck as we watched

the clouds obscure the edges of city blocks.
Finishing our shifts, you and I came home to a

dumb pit bull who stripped the sofa down to the wood
carcass and its cotton guts, happily waiting.

The Universe According to Mongo Santamaria

A telescope as wide as earth to catch photons
slipping out of view in the gravitational

pull that absorbs all into the empty center
is an impossibility, so we set lenses

at a dozen mountaintops waiting for perfect
weather at each simultaneously to find

the edges of the invisible thing that eats
the rules of physics so that all this could be

an illusion and, if true, all history could
rest in the silence before the first chorus of

Willie Bobo's "Evil Ways" at a Detroit house party
in 1979 for the new shop steward.

4.

"Since the unconscious pays tribute to and seeks to preserve archaic forms of psychic meaning—forms of meaning that derive from our family history and early infantile experiences—it can cause us to think and act according to formulas derived from the distant past. These formulas—the emotional rules of engagement that we bring to our interactions with the world, so to speak—may have little to do with our conscious aspirations. Yet they can be potent enough to guide our behavior in life-defining ways."

--Mari Ruti

Bazooka Joe at the Shoe Store

Walking past a construction site and through
the creosote cloud of a childhood
shoe store, a kid embarrassed by the clerk's
gift of a hard square of pink gum wrapped in
a Bazooka Joe comic meant for some
other kid now long gone, leaving the first
kid ashamed to be wanting more than new
shoes, wanting to find more than the broken
pots and untoothed combs buried under the
centuries of ash and mud of textbooks
or the National Geographic map
of Mars circa 1973 meant
for some other kid who is also me
sending letters to the Papaya King
asking of allergens to prepare
for some new kid's birthday party.

Octopus Laqueus

Okinawa Institute researchers are hedging their bets
after studying a sampled 29 cephalopods to see if they
dream like we do. Test subjects were of the nocturnal type –
a species of third-shift octopi who stay up all night
and sleep all day. For a test control, they tickled one
endlessly, taking shifts with a soft-bristled watercolor brush
so he couldn't sleep. They found each of the other
subjects were possibly practicing camouflage
techniques during active sleep as they seemed
to be "...responding to a negative episodic memory,"
as skin tone and texture shifted with recorded pulse rates.
Especially this one pinkish-red guy – he would get up
and stumble about in his sleep, flailing against the tank,
eyes rolled back. I know he was having that one where
they're breaking into your apartment and you have a knife
but can't stab anyone because they're like rubber and
your punches are slow-motioned, absorbed soundlessly
into their pillow guts. And one of them stands waiting
outside your front door which is nothing but a swaying
chain-link fence ready to be pushed down. Your walls
don't even connect. It's like a stage set – in one corner
you can see the hallway outside and in another,
the baseball diamond where you played little league
and everyone's breath smelled like hot dog catsup
because coach only bought when you won, but kept hot Pepsi
in his truck for when you lost. And you had the sense he
didn't like any of you and his wife treated him badly
just from the way she made a ceremonial pile
of pink-smeared Parliaments next to her in the bleachers
like a cold ceremonial pyre waiting for offerings
of brown field mice who sometimes hid in the dark
of the visitors' dugout, closer to the concession stand.
Like she had her own god she kept hid from the coach.

Notes

"There Used to be Communism, But Now There's Just God. So We Pray." –The story of the man taking his father's cooling board is from the oral history, *Voices from Chernobyl* by Svetlana Alexievich.

"The Crime of the Century" -- Maurice Sendak was certain that, as a child, he saw a newspaper photo of the dead Lindburgh baby. He was, decades later, proven correct.

"Pick Poor Robin Clean" – This is the title of one of the few songs written by Geeshie Wiley before she disappeared.

"Composite Sketch with Multiple Witnesses" – the lines, "On Ruination Day, the 14th of April/the iceberg broke and the Okies fled and/ the Great Emancipator took a bullet/ in the back of the head," are based on the Gillian Welch songs, "April the 14th, Part 1" and "Ruination Day, Part 2".

***

Zak Mucha, LCSW, is a psychoanalyst in private practice and president of the Chicago Center for Psychoanalysis. He spent seven years working as the supervisor of an Assertive Community Treatment (ACT) program, providing 24/7 services to persons suffering from severe psychosis, substance abuse issues, and homelessness. Mucha has worked as a counselor and consultant for U.S. combat veterans undergoing training for digital forensic investigations in child pornography. He is also a board member for the Legislative Drafting Institute for Child Protection,

Before going into the clinical field, Mucha has worked as a freelance journalist, truck driver, furniture mover, construction worker, union organizer, staff member at a juvenile DCFS locked unit, and taught briefly at a women's prison. He is the author of *Emotional Abuse: A Manual for Self-Defense*, a previous collection of poetry, *Shadow Box* (Albireo MKG, 2019), and a novel, *The Heavyweight Champion of Nothing* (Dockyard Press, 2021). *Swimming to the Horizon: Crack, Psychosis, and Street-Corner Social Work* (Koehler, 2024).

More can be found at www.zakmucha.com.

Printed in the USA
CPSIA information can be obtained
at www.ICGtesting.com
LVHW062243161223
766680LV00052B/1125